THE ANTI COLORING BOOK

Susan Striker
Edward Kimmel

AN OWL BOOK
HENRY HOLT AND COMPANY / NEW YORK

To Stephen, Howard, and Rachel Kimmel

Special thanks for their help and inspiration to
Herberta W. Sinkus, Herb Perr, John Striker, Joan Imbrogno,
and to all our students, especially John Mengel, Philip Popielarski,
and Peter Popielarski.

"If we pretend to respect the artist at all,
we must allow...freedom of choice....
Art derives a considerable part of its beneficial
exercise from flying in the face of presumptions."

Henry James

Henry Holt and Company, Inc.
Publishers since 1866
115 West 18th Street
New York, New York 10011

Henry Holt® is a registered
trademark of Henry Holt and Company, Inc.

Published in Canada by Fitzhenry & Whiteside Ltd.,
195 Allstate Parkway, Markham, Ontario L3R 4T8.

ISBN 0-8050-0246-4

Henry Holt books are available for special promotions and
premiums. For details contact: Director, Special Markets.

Printed in the United States of America
All first editions are printed on acid-free paper.∞

40 39 38 37 36 35 34 33 32 31 30 29

Grateful acknowledgment is made to Dr. Irene Russell and the
National Art Education Association for permission to use
drawings from Research Bulletin, Vol. 3, No. 1, 1952; and to
Michele Irvin for permission to reproduce her photograph.

Introduction

PICASSO ONCE SAID THAT he wished he could draw as well as a child. This book is intended to set free the child in all of us. Every project is designed to stimulate the imagination and spark creativity, to generate fantasy and expand a child's frame of reference. Most important, there is no uniform solution or correct answer to any of these projects. They encourage flexibility of thinking and fluency of ideas, and it is unlikely that any two individuals will complete a drawing the same way. A child's finished drawing will be intensely personal and highly individual, and, we hope, will represent his or her emotions, intellectual capabilities, physical development, perceptual awareness, interests, and aesthetic tastes.

The artistic impulse is universal. Jackson Pollock said, "Art is a state of being. An artist paints what he [or she] is." Painting something that comes from within fulfills a genuine need. The child who never discovers art as an outlet must seek other forms of expression. The closest many urban youngsters have come to expressing themselves with paint recently has been to spray their names on the sides of subway cars.

For too many children, "art" experiences have been reduced to such passive activities as painting by numbers, coloring, tracing, and "string art." None of these activities approaches the real meaning of art for children: self-expression. Although we have placed our children in front of television sets and offered them only the most passive art experiences, we have not been able to stifle their basic need to express themselves. We must direct that need by providing children with opportunities to participate actively and self-confidently in art activities that stimulate and excite them.

Children who are not given paper will draw on walls or in the sand. At about the age of two, children spontaneously begin to scribble. After a while, they give names to their scribbles and later tell long stories about what these scribbles represent. Young children derive tremendous joy and satisfaction from their art.

Unfortunately, most adults judge a child's drawing by how accurately it depicts reality. They overlook the most significant aspect of early scribblings, the fact that these drawings represent an important stage of artistic development, as well as provide for imaginative thinking. While parents expect their children to crawl before they walk, they don't always see the importance of the various steps of creative activity necessary for all children to develop inventive minds and the ability to think for themselves.

However, we make the mistake of trying to convince children that their drawings must look a certain way in order to be acceptable. We give them coloring books that consist of drawings by highly skilled professional artists; we ask them to abandon their own adventurous journey toward creativity and stay within the lines. By the time they have completed the first few pages of the average coloring book, the only thing they will have learned is that adults draw better, by adult standards, than they do. At this point most children spurn their own refreshing and expressive drawings.

Dr. Irene Russell's classic example is typical of the proof research has uncovered that the imitative procedures found in coloring books rob children of their abilities to think independently and to express their feelings through art. The first drawing (a) shows a child's depiction of a bird before the child was exposed to coloring books. Once asked to copy a coloring book illustration (b), the child lost originality in subsequent drawings of birds (c).

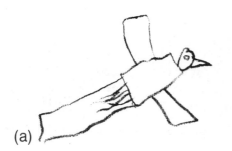
(a)

(b)

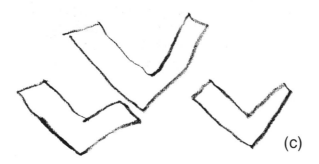
(c)

How accurate a picture looks when completed is of no consequence to a child. The satisfaction comes from the experience of drawing and painting itself. The joy is in actively participating in the art experience.

This book was not written for those rare but fortunate children whose art remains untouched by adult interference. Such children need only blank pieces of paper and their own deeply rooted creative impulses. This book is for anyone who has ever said "I can't draw" or "I don't know what to draw." It is, in effect, an anti-coloring book, designed to help counteract the many other books that promote anti-child activities. We hope to rekindle the excitement of fantasy, to reawaken the senses, and to reaffirm individuality and self-expression. We hope, too, that many adults will rediscover the sense of freedom and adventure that art can give them. Leave your inhibitions behind, and have fun.

You are a space pioneer. Design a flag for your new planet.

The Anti-Coloring Book® / Owl Books

©Striker and Kimmel

A famous artist needs your help. The artist started
this picture but was stung on the thumb by a bee.
Turn the picture any way you'd like and finish it.

FIRST DAY OF ISSUE

Design a postage stamp for the first
letter mailed from Mars.

Name of fish: NEMO

Discovered by: GAVIN MONAHAN

Place discovered: ~~IN~~ UNDER THE SEA In the pet shop

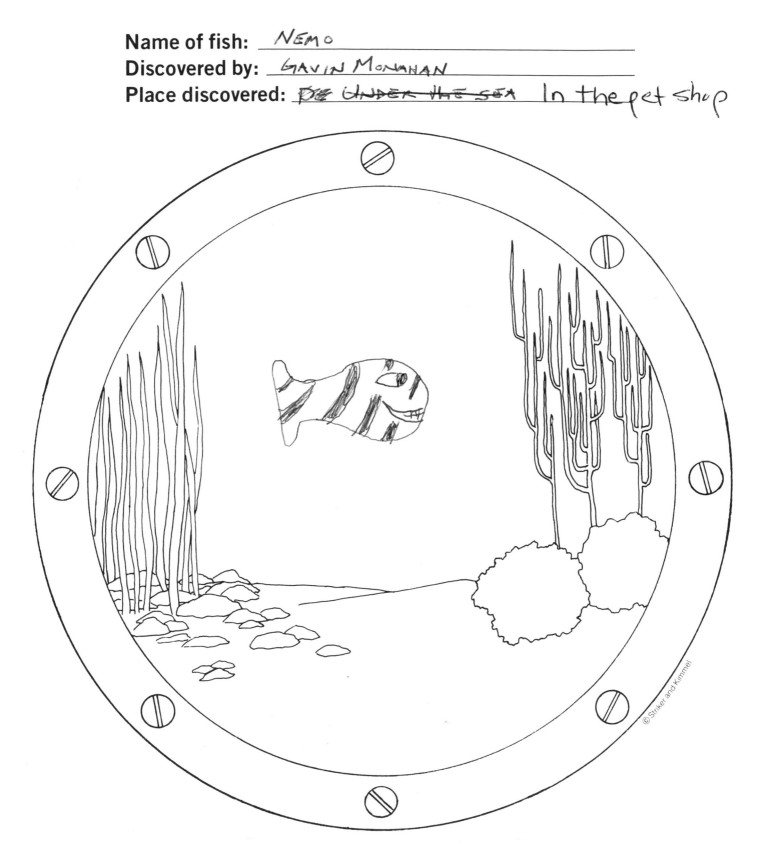

Scientists have just found a new species of fish, but they haven't named it yet. What do you think it looks like and what would you call it?

What was the nicest dream you ever had?

Draw the worst nightmare you ever had.

DAILY
25¢

Vol. 1 No. 1   ©Striker and Kimmel

EXTRA! EXTRA!
MARTIANS LAND

The Anti-Coloring Book® / Owl Books

FUNCTION: _____

_____

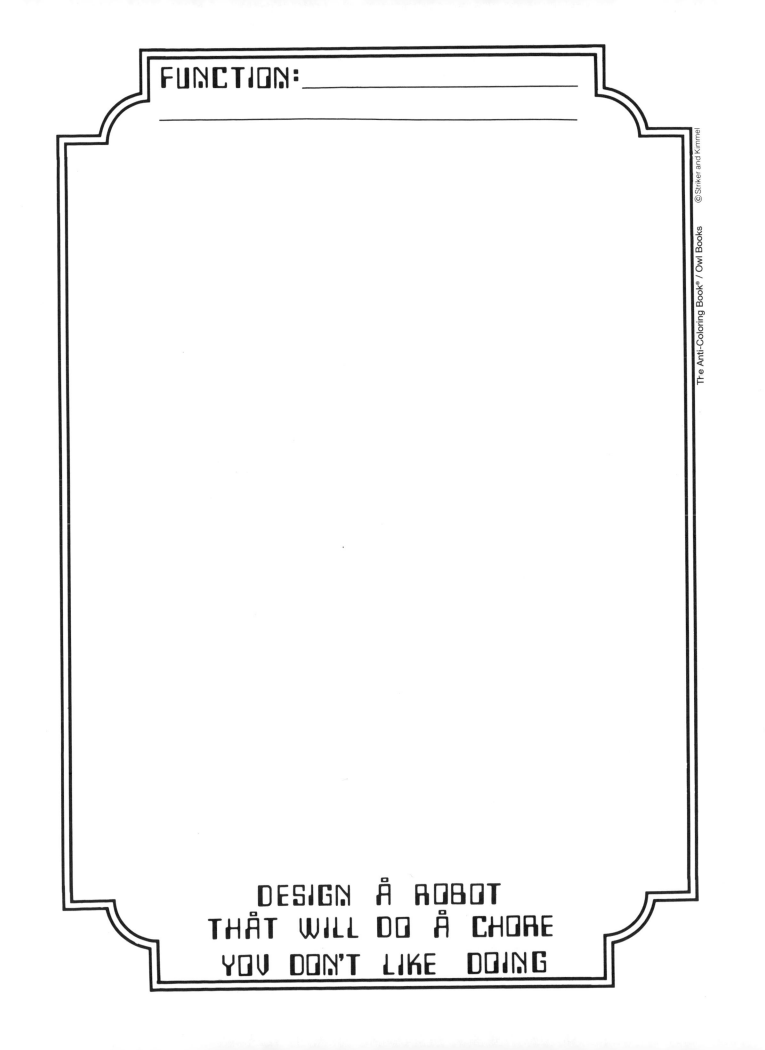

DESIGN A ROBOT
THAT WILL DO A CHORE
YOU DON'T LIKE DOING

The Anti-Coloring Book® / Owl Books

What would you do with one thousand dollars?

Design a shopping bag for the fanciest store in the world.

You are a scuba diver and you have just made the most exciting underwater discovery. What have you found?

What is the photographer taking a picture of?

This clown has learned how to become invisible. We can
see only this circle. What part of the clown do you think the circle is?

Can you change this pair of scissors into something completely different? Turn the paper any way you want to.

©Striker and Kimmel

*Design a family crest that tells something about you
and your family.*

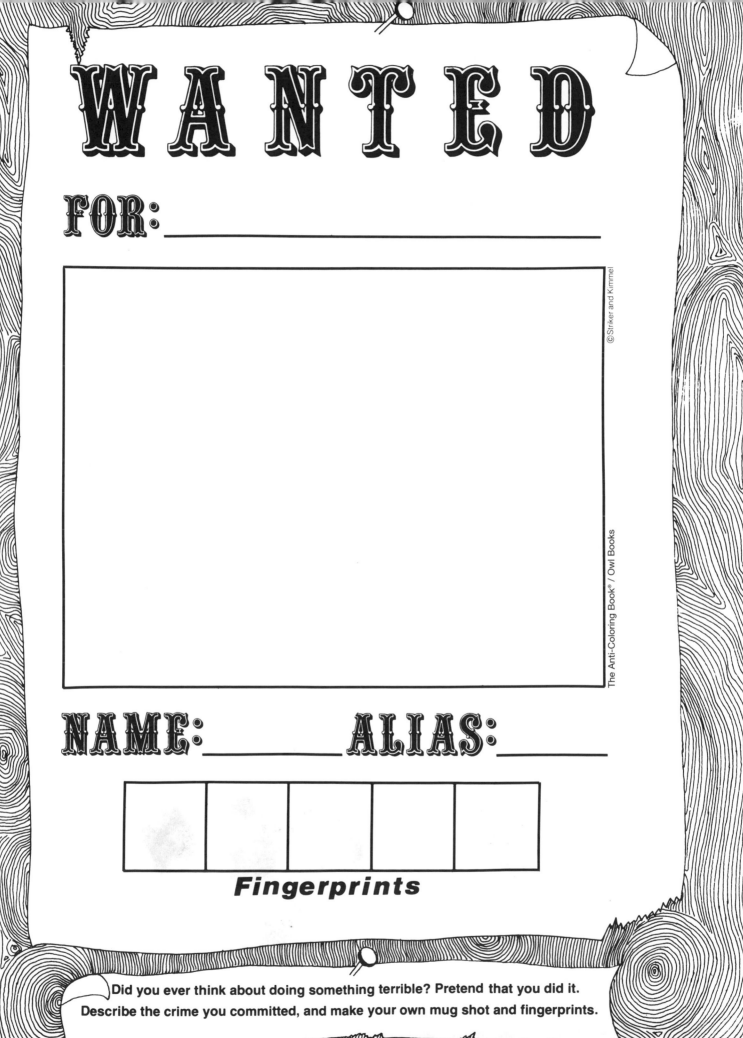

WANTED

FOR: _____

NAME: _____ **ALIAS:** _____

Fingerprints

©Striker and Kimmel

The Anti-Coloring Book® / Owl Books

Did you ever think about doing something terrible? Pretend that you did it. Describe the crime you committed, and make your own mug shot and fingerprints.

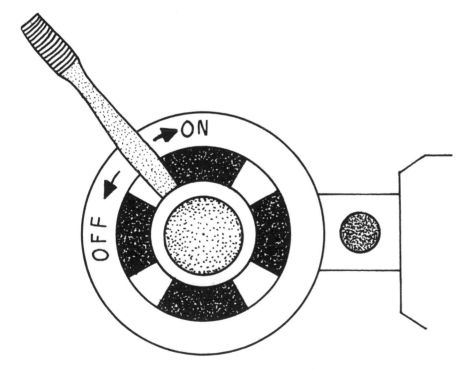

You have just invented a machine that will change
the lives of everyone on earth. Only you understand
the invention well enough to complete the picture.

What would you add to each scene to show the changes in the four seasons?

The Anti-Coloring Book® / Owl Books

Do you see your future in this crystal ball?

TO:

FROM:

© Susan Striker

Today is your birthday. Inside
this box is the present you
want most in the world.
Can you see it?

FLOWER SOCIETY

Name of flower: ⎯⎯⎯⎯⎯⎯⎯⎯⎯⎯⎯⎯⎯⎯⎯⎯
⎯⎯⎯
⎯⎯⎯

Discovered by: ⎯⎯⎯⎯⎯⎯⎯⎯⎯⎯⎯⎯⎯⎯⎯⎯
⎯⎯⎯
⎯⎯⎯

Place discovered: ⎯⎯⎯⎯⎯⎯⎯⎯⎯⎯⎯⎯⎯⎯⎯⎯
⎯⎯⎯
⎯⎯⎯

What does it smell like? ⎯⎯⎯⎯⎯⎯⎯⎯⎯⎯⎯⎯
⎯⎯⎯
⎯⎯⎯

How do you know that it is poisonous? ⎯⎯⎯⎯
⎯⎯⎯
⎯⎯⎯

Size of blossom: ⎯⎯⎯⎯⎯⎯⎯⎯⎯⎯⎯⎯⎯⎯⎯⎯⎯
⎯⎯⎯
⎯⎯⎯

Any other information: ⎯⎯⎯⎯⎯⎯⎯⎯⎯⎯⎯⎯⎯
⎯⎯⎯
⎯⎯⎯
⎯⎯⎯
⎯⎯⎯

You have discovered a poisonous flower growing in your garden. Scientists have asked you to draw a picture of it, name it, and tell something about how you found it.

What are these people looking at?

Where in the world would you like to go to see
a rainbow?

A group of
explorers found a rare bird
deep in the jungle. They sent
back this drawing of the bird
sitting in a tree.

Do you ever lie on your back and imagine that you see pictures in the clouds? What do you see in these clouds?

The Daily Paper

20¢   Vol. 12   No. 24   August 25, 1987

HERO!

You have just performed a heroic deed.
This is the picture and story in the newspaper the next day.

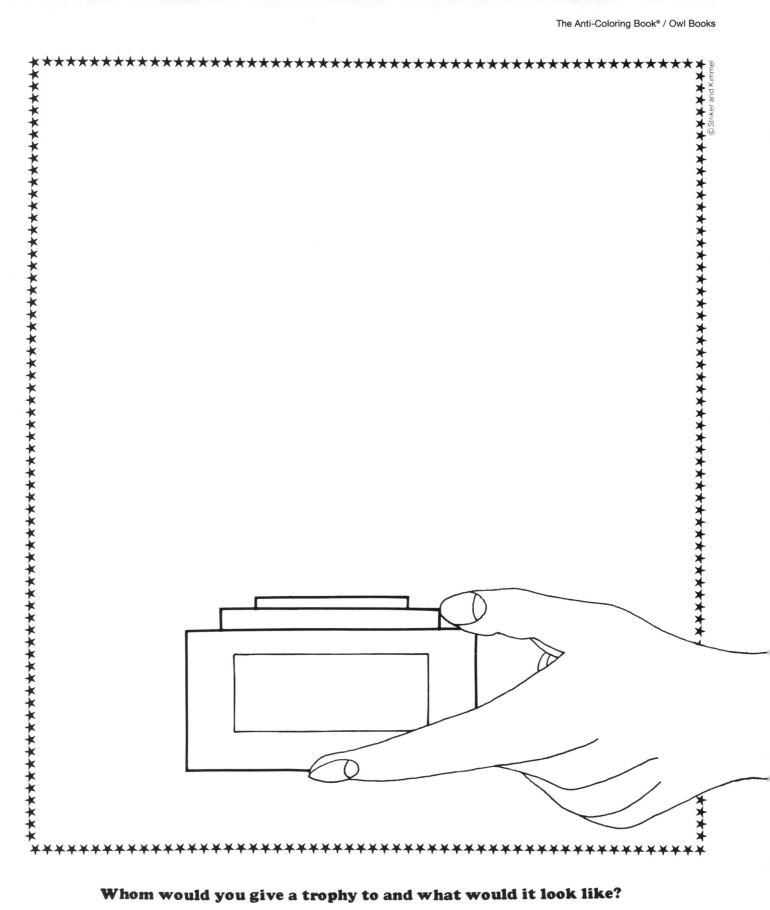

Whom would you give a trophy to and what would it look like?

This man is thinking about how he ended up in jail.

Half of this photograph is missing. Can you complete it?

Some people think there is a man or a woman in the moon, and others say the moon is made of green cheese. What do you think of when you look at the moon?

WHAT DO YOU THINK
GOD LOOKS LIKE?

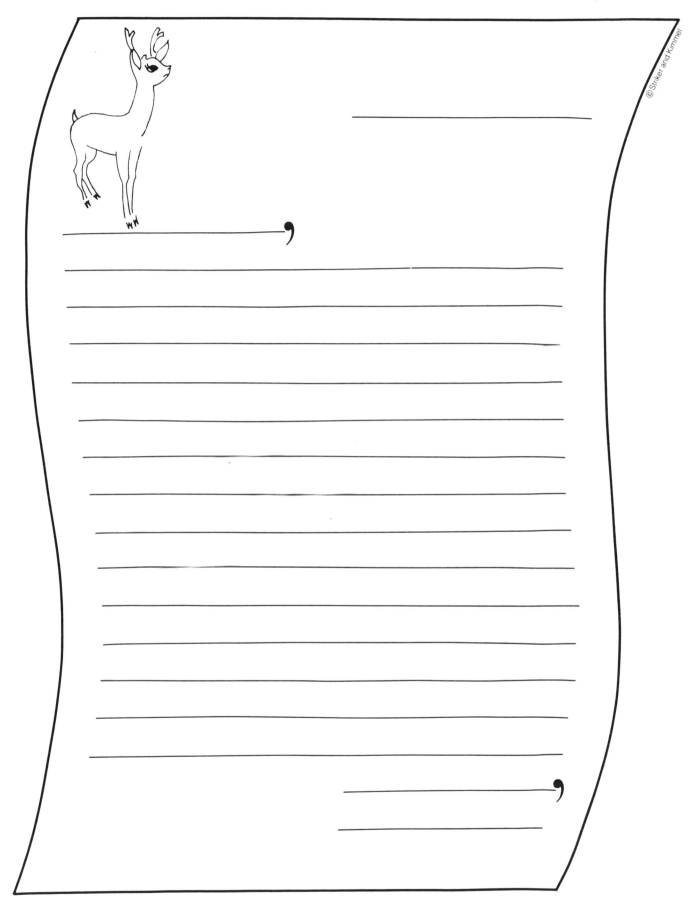

**Write a letter to the person you like (or hate) most in the world.
Use pictures instead of words wherever possible.**

These people can't decide which hats to buy. Can you help them make up their minds?

Space explorers have discovered flowers growing on the
moons of Jupiter. What do they look like?

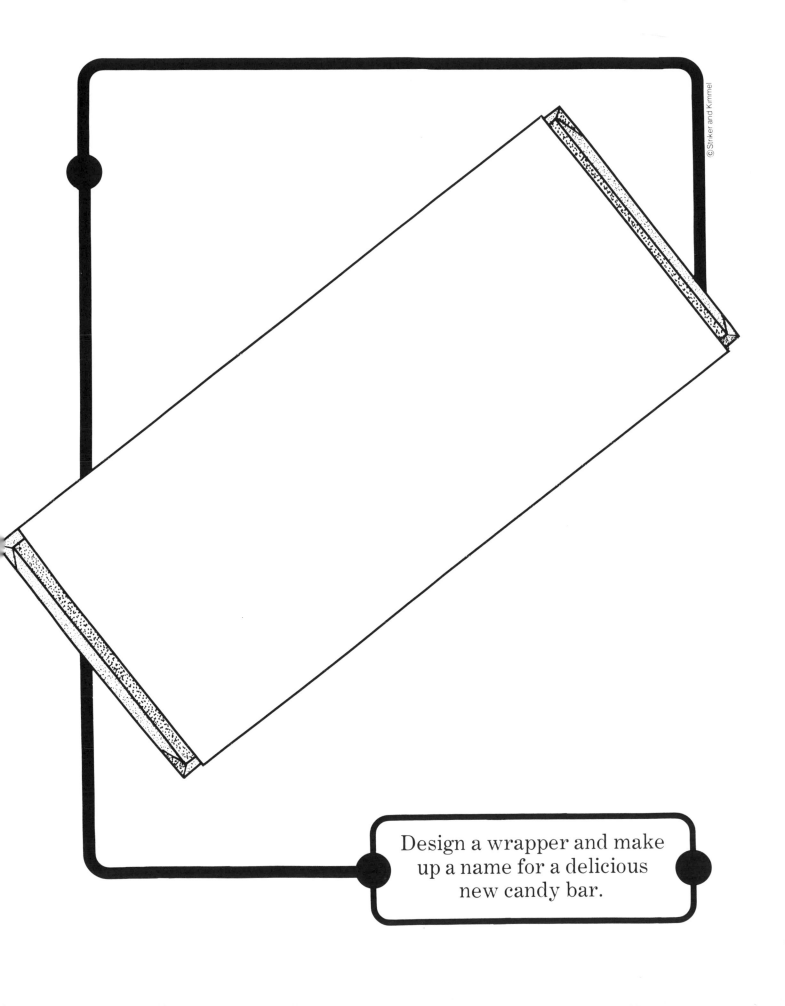

Design a wrapper and make
up a name for a delicious
new candy bar.

©Striker and Kimmel

**What kinds of transportation
will we have in the year 2001?**

What do people do with their faces to show
how they are feeling?

This artist is about to paint a very strange picture. What will it look like?

STAR LIGHT, STAR BRIGHT
FIRST STAR I SEE TONIGHT

I WISH I MAY
I WISH I MIGHT
HAVE THE WISH
I WISH TONIGHT

The Anti-Coloring Book® / Owl Books © Susan Striker

Where are these birds flying to?

The Anti-Coloring Book® / Owl Books

How do you look when you first get up in the morning?

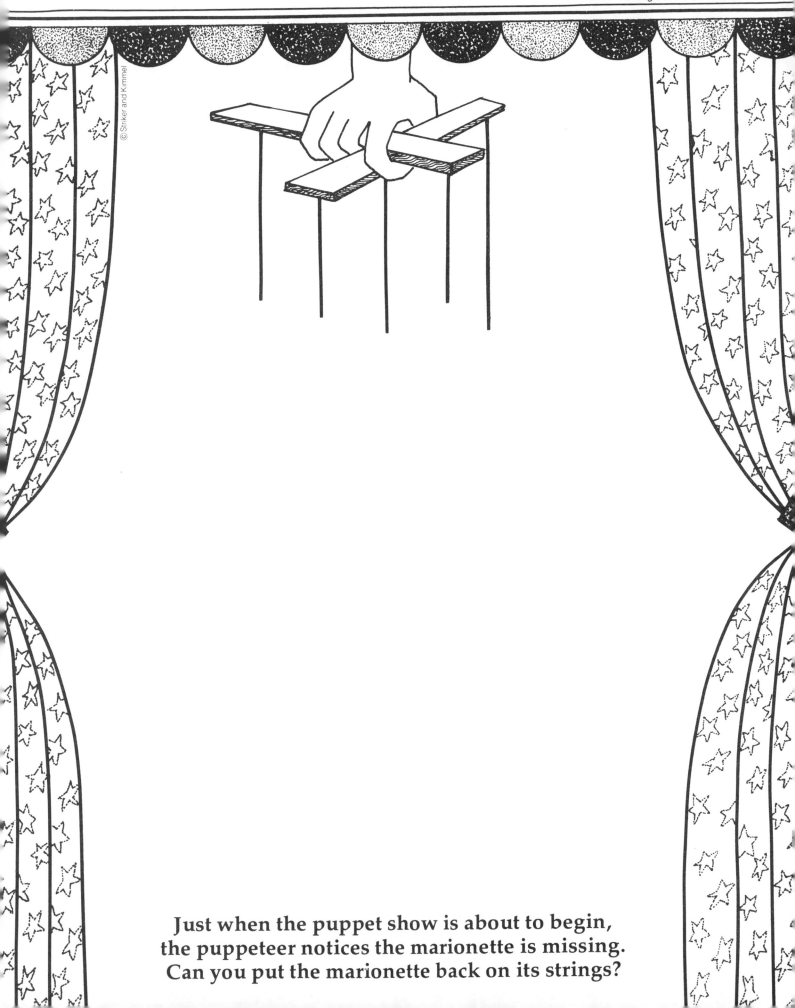

Just when the puppet show is about to begin,
the puppeteer notices the marionette is missing.
Can you put the marionette back on its strings?

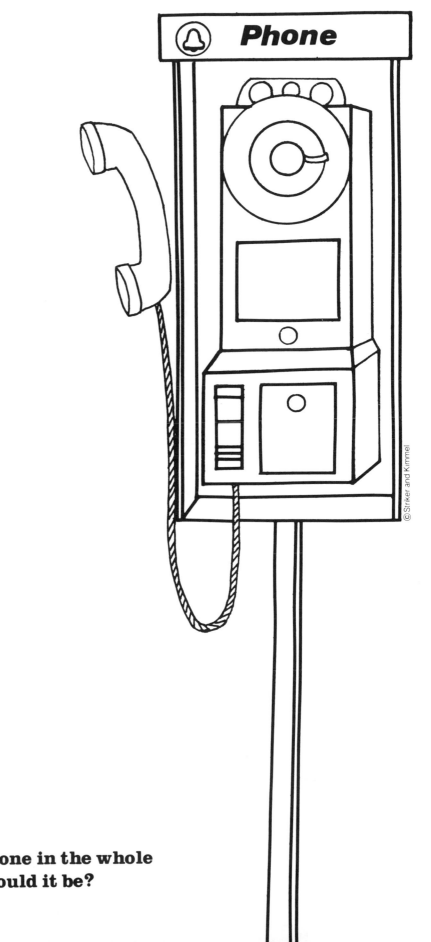

**If you could call anyone in the whole
world, who would it be?**

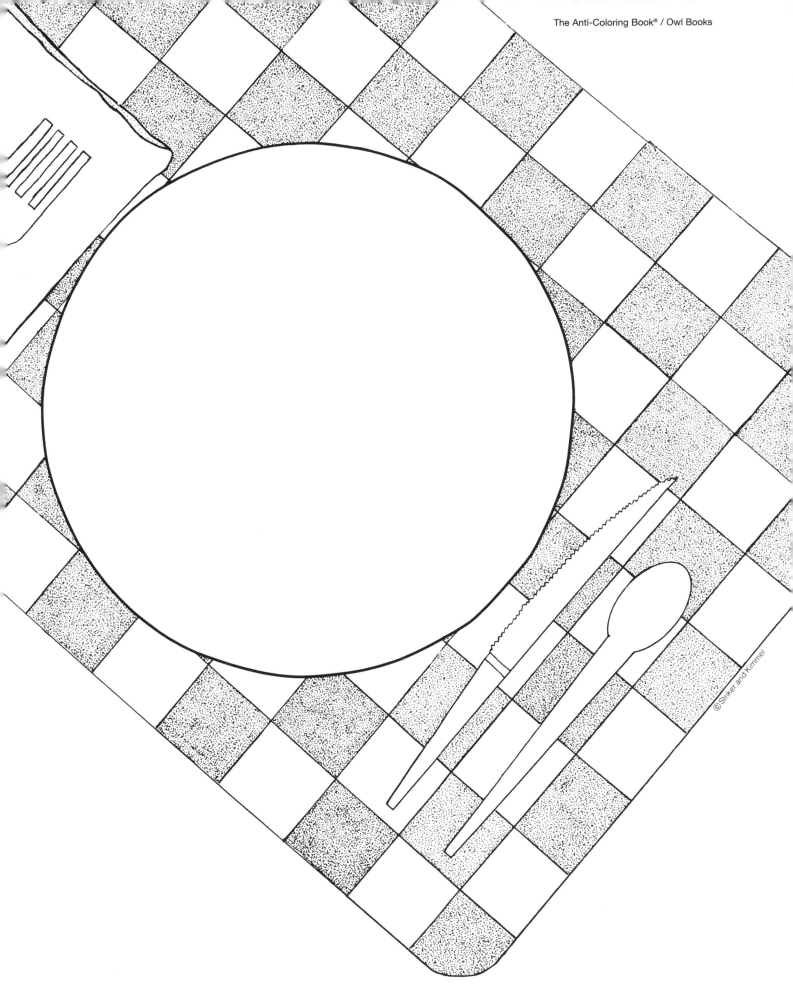

©Striker and Kimmel

Design your own special dinner plate, to be used by you alone.

The Anti-Coloring Book® by Susan Striker and Edward Kimmel
General interest, for ages 6 and older.
ISBN 0-8050-0246-4

The Second Anti-Coloring Book® by Susan Striker with Edward Kimmel
General interest, for ages 6 and older.
ISBN 0-8050-0771-7

The Third Anti-Coloring Book® by Susan Striker
General interest, for ages 6 and older.
ISBN 0-8050-1447-0

The Fourth Anti-Coloring Book® by Susan Striker
General interest, for ages 6 and older.
ISBN 0-8050-2000-4

The Fifth Anti-Coloring Book® by Susan Striker
General interest, for ages 6 and older.
ISBN 0-8050-2376-3

The Sixth Anti-Coloring Book® by Susan Striker
General interest, for ages 6 and older.
ISBN 0-8050-0873-X

The Anti-Coloring Book® of Exploring Space on Earth by Susan Striker
Architecture and interior design.
ISBN 0-8050-1446-2

The Anti-Coloring Book® of Masterpieces by Susan Striker
The world's great art, including color reproductions.
ISBN 0-8050-2644-4

The Inventor's Anti-Coloring Book® by Susan Striker
Inventions, devices, and contraptions.
ISBN 0-8050-2615-0

The Mystery Anti-Coloring Book® by Susan Striker
Mysteries, discoveries, and cops and robbers.
ISBN 0-8050-1600-7

The Newspaper Anti-Coloring Book® by Susan Striker
Write and illustrate your own newspaper.
ISBN 0-8050-1599-X

The Circus Anti-Coloring Book® by Susan Striker with Jason Striker
Clowns, acrobats, and everything else under the big top.
ISBN 0-8050-3412-9

The Anti-Coloring Book® of Celebrations by Susan Striker
Literature-based activities for holidays from around the world.
ISBN 0-8050-3414-5

Artists at Work by Susan Striker
A literature-based Anti-Coloring Book® on careers in art.
ISBN 0-8050-3413-7

Look for these at your local bookstore.